The Complete COMI

Advice on Training, Recovery, Complimentary Nutrition

Joe Arnone, USA Cycling Level 2 Coach

ISBN 978-0-557-55384-6

Table of Contents

Introduction

Hopefully by now you have had time to use your Compex enough to realize you own a very powerful training and recovery tool. As an athlete, it can truly be a secret training weapon. For injury rehabilitation it's not only extremely effective, it can save you a lot of money in potential medical bills. If you enjoy getting an occasional massage, the feeling you get after using the Compex is equal to the best massage you may ever experience.

From first hand experience, I will teach you how to effectively use your Compex to develop training programs, drastically improver your recovery and rehabilitate injuries. In addition, you will learn how to support your Compex usage with cutting edge nutritional advice and the many tips and tricks I've learned over the years.

Regardless of the fact that many resources are available explaining the Compex, I still get questions on a regular basis and much confusion still abounds. How to best place the pads, extend pad life, combine muscle groups, improve strength and endurance among others, are common questions you will find detailed answers to in this book. In your hands is a resource where you can realize all the benefits Compex units have to offer.

The bottom line is your Compex unit is a very valuable resource with benefits you might not fully understand, even after years of use. This book is designed to assist you with getting the maximum benefit from this amazing piece of technology without needing years of use to realize the full potential.

Compex Performance

Chapter One – Compex 101

This basic usage information is specific to the Compex Sport model that I own. The newer U.S. models such as the Sport Elite and Performance, as well as models from other countries like the Mi Sport, Mi Fitness and Energy, are similar enough to make these details useful to you no matter what model you own.

After turning the unit on and selecting OK, the screen display shows the selection of programs. Each program allows you to select body areas depending on the muscle group you are working such as upper or lower body. Other models may allow you to select a more specific muscle group. Some of the programs give you the option of selecting an intensity level from 1-5. This is depicted by the set of stairs. Level 1 is for beginners and initial muscle adaptation. The selections are available for you to progress at your own pace up to the maximum level of 5. The higher the level selected, the longer the muscle contraction and the longer the overall workout in most instances.

The intensity level (displayed in milliamps – mA) indicates the percentage of muscle fibers you are recruiting at a given time in the workout. Intensity is adjusted with each of the four +/- buttons on the face of the unit. During training or competition without using the Compex, you can only recruit approximately 40% of your muscle fibers. Even lifting weights at the maximum weight you are able to achieve, you are only recruiting a maximum of about 40% of your available muscle fibers. Imagine being able to maximize your strength without the risk of injury. With the Compex, you can recruit up to 100% of your muscle fibers, which is immediately evident when you see your first muscle contraction. You will see muscles you didn't know you had!

The benefit of recruiting a higher percentage of muscle fibers during Compex workouts will become obvious when you are engaging in your chosen sport – it will make you faster and stronger, guaranteed!

Level Selection Options and Usage Suggestions

There are a couple of different ways to increase the intensity levels of your workouts with the Compex. Some options are listed below and are offered as a "starting point" that you should customize to fit your specific needs and goals.

1. One level selection option is to progress the intensity on Level 1 up to as high as 100mA, go to the next level, lower the intensity, and then progress to as high as 100mA on this level.

Continue with this method until you reach Level 5 and as high as 100mA. If you choose this method, you don't have to go up one level and decrease the intensity down to the very bottom of the scale. But I do suggest you decrease the intensity at least 20mA for each level increase. Keeping the same intensity and increasing to the next level will most likely result in some muscle soreness.

EXAMPLE:

Week 1

Monday	Wednesday	Friday
Level – 1	Level – 1	Level – 1
Intensity – 10mA	Intensity – 20mA	Intensity – 30mA

Week 2

Monday	Wednesday	Friday
Level – 1	Level – 1	Level – 1
Intensity – 40mA	Intensity – 50mA	Intensity – 60mA

Week 3

Monday	Wednesday	Friday
Level – 1	Level – 1	Level – 1
Intensity – 70mA	Intensity –80mA	Intensity – 90mA

Week 4

Monday	Wednesday	Friday
Level – 1	Level – 2	Level – 2
Intensity – 100mA	Intensity – 80mA	Intensity –90mA...

2. The second option is to work a couple weeks on Level 1 with the intensity in the 10-20mA range for muscle adaptation. Then, stay at the same intensity but go straight to Level 5. As long as you progress the intensity up very gradually, this can be as effective as progressing through each level. This is the method I prefer. My program has always been to increase the intensity by 5mA on the increase week so that you are up 10mA total from the start of the week. The following week I stay at the previous Friday's intensity for the entire week. The next week I progress up another 10mA and continue this progression until I reach my maximum desired intensity.

EXAMPLE:

Week 1

Monday	Wednesday	Friday
Level – 1	Level – 1	Level – 1
Intensity – 10mA	Intensity – 15mA	Intensity – 20mA

Week 2

Monday	Wednesday	Friday
Level – 1 Intensity – 20mA	Level – 1 Intensity – 20mA	Level – 1 Intensity – 20mA

Week 3

Monday	Wednesday	Friday
Level – 5 Intensity – 20mA	Level – 5 Intensity – 25mA	Level – 5 Intensity – 30mA

Week 4

Monday	Wednesday	Friday
Level – 5 Intensity – 30mA	Level – 5 Intensity – 30mA	Level – 5 Intensity – 30mA

Week 5

Monday	Wednesday	Friday
Level – 5 Intensity – 35mA	Level – 5 Intensity – 40mA	Level – 5 Intensity – 40mA...

I've adjusted this method slightly from time to time depending on how I feel. You can increase intensity slightly faster without soreness when you are very fit. If you do get some soreness, back down the intensity and increase a little slower until you can progress again without soreness. Whatever method used is completely your choice. Decide what works best for your specific training goals and adjust as needed.

Like any workout routine, you need to vary your Compex usage depending on where you are in your season. Use each program as it corresponds to the type of workout needed for your specific sport. For example, if you normally do endurance workouts two or three days a week, I suggest you only use the Endurance program on the Compex two or three days a week. I suggest you use the Compex Endurance program OR your normal endurance workout typically. I don't recommend both complete workouts on the same day. This would be too much endurance training in most instances.

You could also use the Compex Endurance program to complete a short workout or to replace a planned workout that didn't happen for some reason. If the weather was bad or some other reason caused you to shorten your workout, you could finish it off with the Compex Endurance program. The same holds true for other strength building programs including Resistance, Strength and Explosive Strength.

Other programs such as Active Recovery, Potentiation and all non strength programs can be used every day if you like and even multiple times per day.

WARNING!: The best advice I can give you is to start at low intensities and gradually work up to higher levels and intensities. Even on Level 5, at an intensity of 10-20mA, it doesn't feel like you are doing much work. You are well advised to stay below 20mA regardless of what you are feeling for at least the first 2 or 3 workouts. Only then should you gradually start increasing the intensity - just don't increase too quickly! You can absolutely destroy yourself requiring weeks to recover if you increase the intensity faster than your muscles adapt. I coached a cyclist that decided to do a Compex Strength workout during his racing season. Being fit he figured Level 5 and 70mA on the intensity would be ok. Two days after he did this, his legs were so sore he said the sheets laying on his legs in bed was painful. It took 2 weeks for the soreness to subside. He destroyed his ability to race the rest of the season.

Program Specifics

The following programs are indicative of any model Compex you may own. Not all units have every program and the names are different depending on the model. These suggestions cover most any program no matter the model however.

Potentiation

In other words, "Warm Up". This is a great program and I highly recommend using it before EVERY competition. You will still need to do some type of cardiovascular warm up as it doesn't raise your heart rate at all. The program is about 3 ½ minutes long and there is NOTHING else you can do to get your muscles warmed up as effectively as you can with the Compex Potentiation program. I used the Potentiation program on my 77 year old father before his yearly Montana Hillclimb race. He had been complaining about how long it took him to warm up. Not only did he feel great but he broke the record he set for his age group several years before. Older athletes in particular will benefit from using Potentiation before any event as it takes longer and longer to warm up for most.

I suggest you use Potentiation in the 30-50mA range initially. As your muscle fibers adapt, feel free to experiment with higher intensities. The very first time you use this feature, you are well advised to start a little lower in intensity and work your way up. This is true for ALL the Compex programs. If you don't follow this advice on the Strength programs for instance, there is a good chance that you will be so sore that you will cry like a baby for a couple days - REALLY!

Endurance

I think this program is the hardest workout you can do with the Compex. The contraction is very long and the rest period is only a couple seconds. On Level 5 (which lasts almost 55 minutes), using this program is equivalent to two hours of running or three hours of cycling.

This feature is very effective used as an addition to your workout that may be cut short due to weather, illness, etc. If you are sick and don't want to do a cardiovascular workout, this can be an excellent muscle workout to help eliminate the possibility of a respiratory infection.

The Endurance program is something you can use during your competitive season as well. You have little chance of getting sore using this program as long as you stay reasonable with the intensity. I used this program very effectively while training for the Tour de Tucson in November 2004. Living in Montana, I'm not able to put in the miles this late in the year so I used the Endurance program to help make up for the lack of miles on the bike. I placed 5th where the previous year without using the Compex I placed 75th.

If you compete in road cycling, cross country mountain biking, triathlon, ultra running or any other endurance sport, you will benefit from using the Endurance program on a regular basis.

Strength

This feature is designed to build pure strength and will definitely build muscle mass. I have never been one to put on much mass with weight training. I have developed more muscle mass and developed it much faster using the Compex than I ever did weight lifting.

I only utilize the strength training programs (Strength, Explosive Strength, Endurance or Resistance) a maximum of 3 days a week. I highly recommend using the Active Recovery at least 3 other days of the week. The very first time you use the Strength program, please start a little lower on the intensity level and work your way up. Again, this is true for ALL the Compex programs - I've said this at least 3 times now so hopefully you get this important message!!!

Any athlete looking to improve pure strength without being concerned with muscle mass increase will benefit from using the Strength program. Sprinters both in running and cycling should use the Strength program extensively.

Explosive Strength

This program is designed to build short burst power and speed. It is ideally suited to pure sprinters. It can be very effective in helping you develop your fast twitch muscles if you have the occasion to sprint in your competitions. I suggest you do this as a block of training after the Strength block.

Golfers and tennis players might also benefit from using Explosive Strength for their upper bodies in particular.

Resistance

This is a very versatile program that is best compared to moderate weight with more repetitions in the gym. It can be used effectively in the following ways:

1. You could use this for 3-4 weeks prior to starting the Strength block to help your muscles get adapted to strength building. This will allow you to start the Strength program at a higher setting and increase the intensity levels quicker without as much muscle soreness.

2. Resistance is an excellent program for strength maintenance. I use the Resistance program during the racing season at a maximum intensity level of 75mA. This helps me maintain advantages I gained during my off season strength program.

3. The Resistance program can also be very effective at building strength without building a lot of muscle mass. If you are concerned about gaining weight from building muscle, the Resistance program is ideally suited to you.

Distance runners, cyclists who are pure climbers, and short track mountain bike racers would all be excellent candidates for using the Resistance program as a primary training tool.

Active Recovery

In my opinion, this program alone pays for your investment. If you get a massage with any regularity at all, you will thoroughly enjoy and appreciate this program. In addition, you will be saving the $50-$100 per hour you pay for a massage. Recovering from your workout is what makes you stronger and faster. Therefore, I recommend using Active Recovery on a regular and frequent basis.

The intensity to use for Active Recovery is is something you can experiment with. Relating this program to a massage, if you want a light massage, I recommend using it somewhere in the range of 25-35mA. If you want a deeper massage, 35-45mA is a good place to start. Most of my sessions are done at 40-50mA now as I have adapted my muscles over time to handle higher intensities. When I'm working out at the higher levels with the strength programs, I start Active Recovery close to the intensity of my workout. I've gotten to 100mA with the Strength program. When I'm working out at 100mA, I start the Active Recovery at 75mA. The intensity increases over the course of the recovery session on it's own. After starting at 75mA, the intensity finishes at close to 100mA.

It is possible to have a little bit of muscle soreness the next day if you use the higher intensities, just like you may have experienced after a deep tissue massage. Most times however, you will only notice a very fresh feeling in your muscles. Just to be safe though, I use a maximum of 35mA when I use Active Recovery the night before a race.

I like to be in a relaxed position when I am doing Active Recovery. I lay on my back when doing muscle groups on the front of the body and lay on my stomach for back, hamstrings, glutes, calves, etc. Quite often, I do this on my couch while watching TV and it relaxes me so much I frequently fall asleep during the program.

Everyone can benefit from using Active Recovery regardless of whether they are an athlete or not. If you know anyone that suffers from chronic muscle aches or that has some sort of muscle injury, you will be doing them a favor by guiding them through an Active Recovery session.

Combining Muscle Groups

It is nice to be able to combine muscle groups so you can shorten the amount of time it takes to complete a workout. I am a cyclist so I have elected to concentrate on my quads, hamstrings and glutes. I use the pad placement book example for my quads and then I have a technique for combining hamstrings and glutes.

Figure 1 shows pad placement graphics for combining glutes and hamstrings:

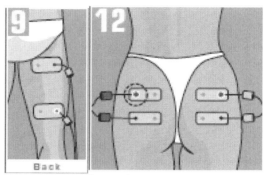

Figure 1

Doing this, I have two large pads on each hamstring and two large pads on each glute as you can see. The large pads have two connectors per pad. I only hook up to one of the connectors on each pad. The positive lead will go on the large pad that is replacing the two small pads and the negative on the other large pad. You could use the same concept to combine quads and calves so you could get a complete leg workout with just two rounds of any program.

CAUTION: For your hamstrings, the pad that is closest to the back of your knee must be positioned correctly. You will notice the tendons behind your knee run up to your hamstring.

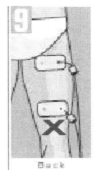

Figure 2

DON'T put the first large pad on the tendons just above the back of your knee. Flex your hamstring and look for where the muscle begins. For me it is about half way between my knee and the bottom of my glute. This is where I place the first pad. The next one is placed just below the bottom of your glute. Figure 2 shows you the area where you SHOULDN'T place the lower pad.

Pad Life

Depending on how your pads are used and stored, you can have very long life or what seems relatively short. One way to tell if your pads are worn out is when you begin to notice a sharp "pins and needles" type of prickling sensation on the skin surface. If you feel this, replace the offending pad immediately. Obviously if the pads won't stick to your muscles, they have run their course as well. Another indication is not being able to increase intensity to your usual levels or ability to increase intensity as quickly as normal. Using pad gel or a drop of water can solve this problem for awhile and help you extend the life of your pads.

In order to extend pad life as long as possible, try this -
1. Apply to shaved areas of the body parts where you are placing the pads if possible.

2. Wash the areas where pads are to be applied with soap and water or rubbing alcohol. If you use rubbing alcohol, use a quality lotion after your Compex session or you will have very dry patches of skin.

3. Make sure the pads are kept in their plastic bags with the zip lock seal tightly closed. To make extra sure they don't dry out, you should store all of your open bags of pads in a larger zip lock bag if you live in a dry climate in particular.

Uneven Twitching
This is something that many Compex users will experience. This will be happening to you if one muscle group twitches or contracts more noticeably than it's counterpart even though both are set to the same level of intensity. For example, let's say you

are doing an Active Recovery routine and you have all four channels (two on each quad) set to the same number of 20mA. However, you notice that your right quadriceps muscle is twitching or shaking quite vigorously while your left is only twitching slightly. This shows you visually that your left leg is weaker than your right.

The weaker muscle is the one that isn't twitching as much. This is due to the fact that a lower percentage of the muscle fibers are responding to the input from motor nerves, whether mentally or electronically activated. The good news is the Compex is the fastest and most effective way to correct uneven muscle strength.

Correcting Your Muscle Imbalance

Up until now, the only way for athletes to correct a muscle strength imbalance was by doing clumsy single limb exercises which are difficult to do and have a pretty high risk of injury associated with them.

It is immediately apparent if you have uneven muscle strength when you use the Compex. If you notice one muscle twitching less than the other when the intensities are equal, you have a strength imbalance. Simply increase the intensity on the low twitching side until both muscles are twitching equally. This is especially effective with the strength programs. You will be able to gradually reduce the difference. It doesn't take very long to correct an imbalance in most cases. After as few as two or three sessions, you will have "awakened" those lazy muscle fibers and may be able to even up the intensity. Once you have each side twitching equally at the same intensity, you will have corrected the imbalance for the most part. Continuing to use the Compex with equal intensities on both sides of your body will assure your strength is the same on your left and right muscle groups.

This chapter has covered most of the basic usage questions many users have. In Chapter 6, I detail some of the tips and tricks I've learned over they years.

Chapter Two – Off Season Training

Using your Compex during the off season is one of it's most effective uses. For example, you can use the strength programs to build muscle mass and strength without ever going to the gym. Additionally, you can build MAXIMUM strength without the risk of injury.

In an effort to provide you with some specific strength training benefits, I have developed a program that is a good starting point for most users. The details are graphed for you later in this chapter. As always, adjust as necessary to meet your fitness level and time constraints.

The design of an off season strength protocol is to build pure strength with expected muscle mass and weight gain. If you are concerned about gaining weight, I recommend the use of Resistance and/or Endurance for building strength without significant muscle mass gains. Distance runners are a good example of the type of athlete that might want to avoid muscle mass gains.

You will see the best results if you place the pads as shown in the pad placement book for your primary muscle group. Secondary groups can be combined with pad placement I described in Chapter 1. As a cyclist, I use the pads as shown for quads utilizing two small pads and one large pad on each leg. I combine glutes and hamstrings with the large pad combination and I have had great results this way. Just be advised that your best muscle fiber recruitment comes with the combination of 2 small pads and 1 large pad as the pad placement guide illustrates.

You can adjust the Off Season Strength Program listed in this chapter to best fit your goals and time constraints. For instance, if you don't sprint in your competitions, you might skip the Explosive Strength cycle and just continue the Strength program for an additional 4 weeks.

Whenever possible, I highly recommend you run the Active Recovery immediately following each session. I often stop the cool down about 5 minutes into it and select Active Recovery while the pads are still in place. You could also skip the 10 minute cool down period all together. All that is required is stopping the program and selecting Active Recovery wherever it's most convenient for you.

Depending on your event and specialty, you can either continue Compex Strength training up to your taper week or switch to another program after 6-8 weeks of this Strength protocol. For endurance cycling, I find it very effective to switch to the Endurance program after my off season strength training. The Compex Endurance program is one of the hardest workouts you will ever do when you get to higher intensities. You can use Endurance throughout the season right up to your taper for your most important events. Experiment with this to find what works best for you and don't be afraid to experiment within the guidelines of caution I've offered.

Off Season Strength Program

This program will consist of:

1. Resistance – 4 weeks – This is a muscle adaptation phase
2. Strength – 8 weeks – For building pure strength and muscle mass
3. Explosive Strength – 4 weeks – To develop sprint strength

BLUE = Increases in Intensity (mA)

RED = Increases in Level (1-5)

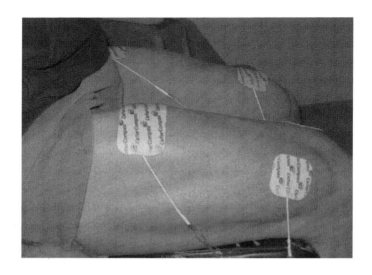

Joe Arnone - Compex 85mA

Adaptation Phase

Resistance – Week 1

Monday	Wednesday	Friday
Level – 1	Level – 1	Level – 1
Intensity – 10mA	Intensity – 10mA	Intensity – 10mA

Resistance – Week 2

Monday	Wednesday	Friday
Level – 1	Level – 1	Level – 1
Intensity – 15mA	Intensity – 20mA	Intensity – 20mA

Resistance – Week 3

Monday	Wednesday	Friday
Level – 5	Level – 5	Level – 5
Intensity – 10mA	Intensity – 10mA	Intensity – 10mA

Resistance – Week 4

Monday	Wednesday	Friday
Level – 5	Level – 5	Level – 5
Intensity – 15mA	Intensity – 20mA	Intensity – 20mA

Strength Building Phase

Strength – Week 1

Monday	Wednesday	Friday
Level – 5	Level – 5	Level – 5
Intensity – 10mA	Intensity – 10mA	Intensity – 10mA

Strength – Week 2

Monday	Wednesday	Friday
Level – 5	Level – 5	Level – 5
Intensity – 15mA	Intensity – 20mA	Intensity – 20mA

Strength – Week 3

Monday	Wednesday	Friday
Level – 5	Level – 5	Level – 5
Intensity – 25mA	Intensity – 30mA	Intensity – 30mA

Strength – Week 4

Monday	Wednesday	Friday
Level – 5	Level – 5	Level – 5
Intensity – 35mA	Intensity – 40mA	Intensity – 40mA

Strength – Week 5

Monday	Wednesday	Friday
Level – 5	Level – 5	Level – 5
Intensity – 45mA	Intensity – 50mA	Intensity – 50mA

Strength – Week 6

Monday	Wednesday	Friday
Level – 5	Level – 5	Level – 5
Intensity – 55mA	Intensity – 60mA	Intensity – 60mA

Strength – Week 7

Monday	Wednesday	Friday
Level – 5	Level – 5	Level – 5
Intensity – 65mA	Intensity – 70mA	Intensity – 70mA

Strength – Week 8

Monday	Wednesday	Friday
Level – 5	Level – 5	Level – 5
Intensity –75mA	Intensity –80mA	Intensity – 80mA

Sprint Strength Phase

Explosive Strength – Week 1

Monday	Wednesday	Friday
Level – 5	Level – 5	Level – 5
Intensity – 30mA	Intensity – 30mA	Intensity – 30mA

Explosive Strength – Week 2

Monday	Wednesday	Friday
Level – 5	Level – 5	Level – 5
Intensity – 35mA	Intensity – 40mA	Intensity – 40mA

Explosive Strength – Week 3

Monday	Wednesday	Friday
Level – 5 Level	Level – 5 Level	Level – 5
Intensity – 45mA	Intensity – 50mA	Intensity – 50mA

Explosive Strength – Week 4

Monday	Wednesday	Friday
Level – 5	Level – 5	Level – 5
Intensity – 55mA	Intensity – 60mA	Intensity – 60mA

a. **Compex Sport "Strength" Program 2010**

I did a 3 month off season strength program during the 2010 winter season using my Compex Sport. I ran this program on my quads only. As you can see by the table, my muscle mass gain was pretty significant and visually noticeable in Figure 3.

I've been able to get out on the bike early this year and I already feel late season strength in my pedaling. I'm continuing to run the strength program at 100mA for a few more months. I will then switch to Endurance for the remainder of the season and see how well I do with this protocol.

Age: 48

Starting Weight: 170 lbs

Ending Weight: 175 lbs

Date	Left Leg	Right Leg	Level	Intensity	Comments
01/18/10	20.5 inches	20.75 inches	1	10mA	No Soreness
01/20/10			5	10mA	No Soreness

01/22/10				5	15mA	Some Soreness
01/25/10				5	20mA	Slight Leftover Soreness at start from 1/22 session
01/27/10				5	20mA	Very Slight Leftover Soreness
01/30/10				5	20mA	No Soreness
02/01/10				5	25mA	No Soreness
02/03/10				5	30mA	No Soreness
02/05/10				5	35mA	No Soreness
02/08/10				5	40mA	Mild Soreness
02/10/10						Too sore for strength. Did active recovery
02/11/10				5	25mA	Got to 30ma had to back down due to soreness
02/13/10				5	30mA	Slight Leftover Soreness at start from 2/8 session
02/15/10				5	35mA	Slight Leftover Soreness at start from 2/13 session

02/17/10			5	40mA	No Soreness
02/19/10			5	40mA	No Soreness
Weight 172	21.25 inches	21.25 inches			
02/22/10			5	45mA	No Soreness
02/24/10			5	50mA	No Soreness
02/26/10					Too sore for strength. Did active recovery
02/27/10			5	50mA	No Soreness
03/02/10			5	55mA	No Soreness
03/04/10			5	60mA	Slight soreness next day
03/08/10			5	60mA	No Soreness
03/10/10			5	60mA	No Soreness
03/12/10			5	60mA	No Soreness
03/15/10			5	65mA	No Soreness
03/17/10			5	70mA	No Soreness
Weight 173	21.75 inches	21.75 inches			

03/19/10			5	70mA	No Soreness
03/22/10			5	75mA	No Soreness
03/24/10			5	80mA	No Soreness
03/26/10			5	80mA	No Soreness
03/29/10			5	85mA	No Soreness
03/31/10			5	90mA	Slight Leftover Soreness at start from last session
04/02/10			5	90mA	No Soreness
04/05/10			5	95mA	No Soreness
04/07/10			5	100mA	No Soreness
04/09/10			5	100mA	
04/12/10			5	100mA	
04/14/10			5	100mA	
04/16/10			5	100mA	
Weight 175	22.0 inches	22.0 inches			

Here is a visual representation of my muscle mass gains. As you can see it's obvious that my quads are much larger at the end of the training then when I started.

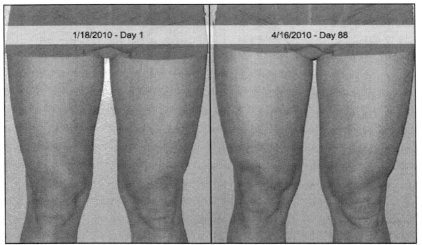

Figure 3

The off season is the time to work on your weaknesses so you can start the next season better prepared. The Compex will once again be a valuable tool for you to accomplish all your goals.

Chapter Three – In Season Training

During the competitive portion of my cycling season, my Compex is still a training and recovery tool that I use regularly. If you aren't using Active Recovery daily, you are putting yourself behind where you could be. I suggest you use your Compex for the following purposes during your racing season.

Active Recovery

I use this program after every long or hard training day. My weekly usage averages 4 – 5 sessions. I've even used it multiple times a day. I also use it frequently for injury prevention and rehabilitation that I detail more in Chapter 4.

The Active Recovery program is most effective used immediately after your workout or race. Try to plan the time so you can do this as soon as possible after a workout. If you have any oils, lotion or sunscreen, either wipe off the area thoroughly or shower before your session. This will help increase the life of your pads. Be sure to revisit other pad life tips listed in Chapter 1.

Your primary muscle groups – the ones that get the most fatigued – should always be recovered. Time permitting, I suggest you use Active Recovery on every other muscle group you have time for.

Active Recovery is divided into 3 distinct benefits through it's 24+ minute program. The first portion is capillary action which increases blood flow through the area. The second portion is endorphin release for pain regulation. The final portion is relaxation. All three are very important for your training and racing recovery. As a matter of fact, Active Recovery lowers your blood lactate level better than anything else you can do – even massage. With so many benefits, it's crazy not to incorporate Active Recovery into your routine as much as possible.

Potentiation

Especially as you age, warming up seems to take longer and longer. Wouldn't it be great to find a way to warm up your muscles without tiring yourself for your race effort? Well that is exactly what the Potentiation program does.

The program only takes about 3 ½ minutes but it makes your muscles feel like you have been using them for 2 hours or more. No cardiovascular warm up benefit comes from using the Potentiation program. However, as far as muscle warm up, it's unbeatable.

For cycling, I'll warm up my legs completely in just 2 sessions. I accomplish this doing quads and calves seated in a chair using the large pad combination and hooking up just one side. I then do glutes and hamstrings together in the same manner but laying on my stomach. Then, all I need to do is get my heart rate up with a couple short efforts on the trainer and I'm more warmed up than riding the trainer for 45 minutes or more. That's a HUGE benefit to your racing!

Endurance, Resistance or Explosive Strength

Depending on the type of athlete you are, one or more of these programs can be very effective during your racing season. You can use any of these or a combination of them up to about a week before your most important events of the season.

Being an endurance cyclist, I use the Endurance program twice a week during the racing season. This allows me to ride fewer miles during endurance days and spend some time at home using the Compex. The benefit you get as far as increased oxygen utilization is very noticeable. I notice after only a few sessions that I'm better able to ride hard up short hills and my legs stay powerful all the way up the hill. This was one of my weaknesses before I discovered Compex so I definitely benefit from this during the season.

I don't have the opportunity to race on the velodrome anymore due to where I live. If I did, I would use the Resistance program at least once a week as well. This targets both fast and slow twitch muscles so it's great for those events where you use both. Track cycling pursuit racing and the 1 mile run are both great examples of events where Resistance can be beneficial for you.

Most every athlete has the need for more explosive quickness. Explosive strength can give you that edge when you are sprinting for the finish or need that quick "pop" to any muscle group.

I suggest you experiment with these programs during your less important events of the competitive portion of your season. You have nothing to lose and very much to gain using the Compex in this manner to give you an additional edge over the competition who isn't.

Chapter 4 – Injury Rehabilitation

The area where my Compex has paid for itself many times over has been for rehabilitating injuries. I continue to be amazed every time I need to use my Compex for an injury. Without it, I would have spent more money and more time trying to get over injuries I've sustained. My Dad and my brother have had similar experiences so you can be certain the injury rehabilitation benefit is extensive.

I use the Active Recovery program and I'm just careful to only increase the intensity a little at a time. I've never had any problems with aggravating an injury. Because of this fact, I'm not afraid to increase intensity higher as my rehabilitation progresses. The newest Compex units have other programs that aren't as intense for the most serious injuries. The Massage program on the Sport Elite unit for example would be very useful for most injuries.

The first injury I experienced where I used my Compex was from a ski accident. I did a high speed cartwheel down the slope and injured my ribs. I didn't get an x-ray so I'm not sure if I had broken ribs or not. The pain was some of the most severe of any injury I have ever experienced however.

What I learned after 3 or 4 days of suffering was the muscles between my ribs were "cramping" to the point it was excruciating. Unlike any other muscle cramp I've experienced, these cramps lasted for hours on end. I tried everything, even muscle relaxers with very little if any relief. I finally wised up and tried my Compex on the area. Unbelievable! It eased the cramps better than anything else I tried. The cramping returned periodically, but every time I used my Compex, it relieved the cramp and the pain immediately.

The next injury I suffered was a severely sprained ankle. I rolled it getting out of a truck and I heard the pop! I went to the doctor to get it x-rayed and they found it severely sprained and not broken, thankfully.

The doctor put me in a soft boot cast to get home and said it would be 3 to 4 weeks before I would be able to put weight on it. I took Ibuprofen right after it happened and then didn't take any kind of pain killer after that.

The day after it happened, I looked in the Compex pad placement guide to see what I could do. I found I could bridge the ankle with two large pads and work the area without any additional pain. I used it twice a day for 3 days. On the fourth day, I rode my bike to the doctor and they returned me to work status! Being able to reduce the healing time from 3 or 4 weeks to 4 days makes a huge difference if you aren't able to work.

Here are pictures I took on day one and then again on day four. Notice the significant difference in the swelling:

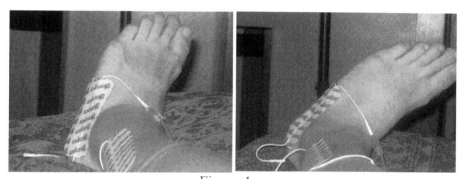

Figure 4

Ankle Sprain Day 1   Ankle Sprain Day 4

The most recent injury I struggled with is a groin strain of some sort. It seems to be tendinitis from all I can tell. Once again, the only relief I get is from using Active Recovery on the area. I keep irritating it with my cycling training but I'm able to manage if effectively with the Compex.

Here is how I place the pads to work this area:

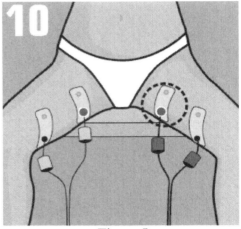

Figure 5

I'm confident most injuries can be rehabilitated with the Compex recovery programs. Look in your pad placement book the next time you are injured, find what looks to work the area, and use it to enhance your rehabilitation. You'll recover faster and you could potentially save thousands of dollars.

Chapter Five – Nutritional Support

Being a competitive athlete most of my life required me to pay attention to nutrition and supplementation. I've learned a lot over the years so I want to offer some suggestions here. Supporting your training with good nutrition could be another integral part of your success or failure.

Food

What you eat as well as when you eat plays a major role in how you perform and recover. Eating a typical American diet will degrade your performance gradually over the years. With all the time, effort, and money you spend training and competing, you owe it to yourself to pay close attention to your diet. I've found just recently that a plant based diet will enhance athletic performance more than I ever thought possible. I highly suggest you start incorporating more fresh, uncooked plant based food into your diet if you don't already.

The primary reason for doing this as an athlete, is to improve your strength and endurance while simultaneously speeding recovery. When I started eating this way, I noticed an immediate improvement to my overall performance and recovery as a cyclist. Then, when I would revert back to the occasional "typical" meal of animal based protein and fat, I felt decreased strength and cardiovascular function.

I'm not a vegetarian or vegan and I don't feel you need to be this "concerned" with never again eating a morsel of animal based food. My problem with the words vegetarian and vegan are the pressure they appear to put on those claiming this title. One of my food philosophies is worrying about what you eat will kill you faster than happily enjoying whatever diet you choose - within reason of course. Putting a title to your food choice style only adds pressure for you to conform, causing undue stress in my opinion. Rather than put a new title to my suggested diet change, I describe it as a diet where I consume more raw, plant based foods; sometimes completely and other times not.

The second, and really most important reason to change your diet in this manner, is due to the fact it could kill you if you don't. Even as a fit looking athletic type your arteries could be getting progressively more clogged with plaque. This puts you at risk of heart disease and a potentially lethal heart attack or stroke. Plaque builds up in your arteries from eating animal based proteins and fats. Even the most fit endurance athletes are at risk. Because of this, you can also see how this could degrade your cardiovascular output as your arteries become more clogged over time.

I'm of Italian heritage and I never thought I would be convinced to do something along these lines as my "love" relationship with food was very strong. Therefore, if I can do it, anyone can. I get just as much enjoyment, and I'd say even more now, preparing meals incorporating more fresh fruits, vegetables and whole grains into my diet.

Supplements

Depending on your eating habits, supplements you require can vary greatly. I've found from personal experience that eating healthier reduces the need I feel for more supplementation. There are some supplements that I feel are needed and effective regardless of your diet choices however.

As an athlete and Compex user, one of your concerns is ammonia production. Typically, athletes desire and will consume more protein than non athletes. Breaking down this protein, and any muscle cannibalism will at times produce more ammonia than your body can get rid of. Stage racers in cycling have noticed this for many years. Taking a supplement that can scavenge excess ammonia in such instances becomes necessary.

Due to my personal need for this as a cyclist, Health and Performance Source manufactured a supplement called Fatigue Fighter. Not only does it scavenge the ammonia as thoroughly as possible, other ingredients add some performance benefit too.

A combination B vitamin supplement is also very good for enhancing your recovery. If you take a quality multi vitamin, it should have enough B vitamins to assist you in this regard. Buying low quality supplements of any kind will most likely negate the potential benefits however, so remember that very often you get what you pay for. One thing to look for in a good multi vitamin is Biotin. It should contain a minimum of 100% of the RDA of Biotin to assure your metabolism of other B vitamins.

It's also useful to know that B vitamins are water soluble. This means they process through your body fairly quickly. If you are taking a good quality B vitamin supplement or multi vitamin, you will notice bright yellow colored urine. This is normal and is further evidence the B vitamins are processing through your system quickly. It also indicates that dosing out your B vitamins, especially on recovery days can be more beneficial than taking them all at once. I typically take my multi vitamin "after" training or racing to further assist with my recovery.

If you are vegan, you will need to supplement with vitamin B-12 about 3 years after you change your diet. Your body reserves will get depleted at some point as the only natural source of B-12 comes from animal sources. Some cereals and yeasts are fortified with B-12 but counting on that as your source probably isn't the best option.

Vitamin D is also important and something more people are becoming deficient in these days. Most athletes spend enough time in the sun that this shouldn't be a problem. If you live in a climate during the winter where you don't see the sun much, you might consider a D vitamin supplement.

Other than that, supplements are really only needed if you feel you have a deficiency of some sort. Certain natural performance enhancing supplements can be good but quality is questionable in many of them. The last thing you want to do is test positive for doping from a supplement that wasn't manufactured with the care and attention you deserve. You spend too much time, effort and money training to have your hard work taken away from you by negligence on someone else's part. Research your supplements thoroughly.

Chapter 6 – Tips and Tricks

Consider this chapter the FAQ section of this book. I've used the Compex for over 7 years so I've learned some very useful tips and tricks that will help you and prevent learning the hard way.

The Unit

As I've said, I use the Compex Sport model. I've also tried the Fitness Trainer and the Sport Elite models so this will cover most any model you own.

Turning the unit on and figuring out how to get started is pretty self explanatory. When you are using a program and increasing or decreasing intensity, there are a few things that are nice to know. With the older models – Sport and Fitness Trainer – adjusting intensity is done one channel at a time. The newer models have a selection where you can choose how to adjust intensities. It's pretty handy to be able to adjust ALL channels with one button.

For the older models, I find it easiest to adjust intensities two channels at a time. For this reason, I connect the two leads on the left to my left leg and the two on the right to my right leg. It's ok to criss cross the leads in any manner you choose. If you don't increase intensity using the two buttons for one muscle however, it will feel a bit strange to stimulate contractions on half the muscle at a time.

One handy technique I've learned is pushing the power button ONCE to pause my workout. If I need to answer the phone, get the door or have another reason to pause, pushing the power button once gives you a pause to the workout. To start again, all you have to do is increase the intensity on a channel and the workout starts where you left off. You'll have to adjust each channel to get back to your desired intensity but then you are right back at it.

CAUTION: Be careful that you don't push the power button again after the first time. If you do this, the program will stop and you'll have to start over.

The battery has great life as I've used mine for up to 2 weeks before needing to recharge it. When the battery indicator shows about $1/16^{th}$ charge remaining, I will plug it in to recharge the battery. The Sport Elite and Performance models are a bit different in the battery life indicator. You'll have to experiment with it to see what indication is best for recharging. It's better to recharge when you have some life left in the battery. It's frustrating to have your workout cut short due to the battery going dead.

I've owned my Sport model for about 7 years. I haven't had to replace the leads or the battery yet. I take care to unplug the pads gently and I only charge the battery when it's nearly dead. These two things have helped prolong the life. Also realize the Sport and Fitness trainer models can be charged with the leads in place. The Sport Elite and Performance models must have ALL leads removed as the charging pin is only exposed by sliding a protector over each lead connection point.

Pads

The pads are about the only recurring cost you'll incur owning a Compex. There are some things you can do to extend pad life, some of which I covered in Chapter One. There are a few other tricks I've learned regarding pad placement and life.

One of the ways I extend the life of my pads and maximize my workout and recovery is to combine the workout and recovery programs as I detailed in Chapter 2.

Something you will experience at some point is the inability to increase intensity to your desired level. You'll notice sometimes you can increase intensity rapidly and other times, the unit will stop you and give you a down arrow indicator.

I've found this results from a couple of different issues. One, after a long ride, I'm frequently low on fluid and electrolytes, especially when it's hot. This is actually a valuable tool for your training. If you try to run Active Recovery after your workout and you can't increase the intensity like normal, it's telling you to drink more water after your workout and get some electrolytes in to assist with your recovery. The second reason is lack of moisture between the pads and your muscles. My trick to solve either issue is to turn the unit off, put a drop of water on your finger and slightly wet each pad. Reapply the pads, start your program and you shouldn't have any other problems. My Dad is 78 and he frequently had this problem. I told him about the water technique and it completely solved it for him. Older muscles typically don't conduct as well so this is a great tip for older athletes in particular.

The last trick, that helps with the older style pads especially, is to connect the leads BEFORE I place the pad on my muscle. This is a handy technique for hard to reach muscle groups when nobody is around to assist you. Glutes are a perfect example. In order to place the pads where they need to be, connecting them before you place the pad is very helpful and sometimes the only way to accomplish the task. Using the newer snap pads makes this technique moot but it may still come in handy depending on the muscle group you are working.

Conclusion

I hope this book helped you learn more about the Compex,
without it taking you years of use to learn them like it did me.
The primary benefit to you will be more time now to experiment
with training techniques that perfectly suit you and your goals.
The beauty of the Compex is the nearly limitless combination of
training programs. Just because your competitors use one,
doesn't mean you can't find a way to beat them at the game.

Probably the best advice I can give you at this point is to use
your Compex as much as possible. The difference between
winning and placing somewhere behind the winner, could very
well come down to how much you utilize your Compex for
training, racing and recovery. It's a tremendous benefit being able
to train and recovery in the comfort of your home. Good luck!

Printed in Great Britain
by Amazon